IF No One Told You...

Your Reflection in Words.

Written by:

Franzioli J. Bastidas

First Things First

1: If we awaken with Happiness in our hearts, we set the stage for a beautiful day.... And why not that? Why wake yourself up with doubt about things that haven't projected negatively its almost self-sabotage and quite funny that you could wake up and chose anger over happiness. don't you think? After all doubt is simply the recipe for fear and fear is just the fuse for anger that ignites what? Doubt! Sound crazy! well it is! So, stop that! chose to be happy everything else will align to that rhythm.

<u>You Are Amazing!</u>

2: Why do you need the validation from them? Don't you realize when you look in the mirror the person looking back is validation? Seeking validation from others is just mirroring for each of us are guilty of it so it's a mirrored distorted view of what validation means. Validation is really the simple belief in what one's idea is apply that respectfully and Bye Bye the need for Validation. It's Ok if No one gets it Those who matter don't mind and those that mind doesn't matter! Respectfully!

<u>*Must Be Tired After All That Judgement*</u>

3: If the judgement is harsh and without proper experience in the subject well like a boomerang it's like you're playing handball with your face! Taking the weight of judging someone for their walks in life without having the same mind, body and soul which no two individuals are the same is simply disrespectful stay in your lane. Think about it how can someone other than thy self-know what it's like except for the one who is dealing!? Don't do this, it's arrogant! and ugly!

Perfection Does Not Exists!

4: Make no Mistake is a Mistake! You are not perfect except in your own eyes and that's a big game the mind likes to play with the ego it sets the tone for pride to come into our perception and weigh it on one sided value. Remember the notion that we are exempt from learning every day and growing is unconstitutional and against the laws of life! it's like being robbed except you're the robber! Just be open, to receive it and organize it later! There is no deadline!

<u>*Is It Worth It??*</u>

5: Is it Everlasting? If you think of an everyday rhythm in life, what does it consist of, and literally can you have it apart of your lifetime and time again? will it stay ripe or rot and become stale and dead like a weed will it consume you or bloom you. Roses are red violets are blue is really the simplest choice of the two everything has an expiration date except Belief. So, what do you believe can withstand the test of time? Is it love? Is it money? Success? When you break down the meanings of each of these options divide that by the time it will be in your life what gave more comfort and joy?

<u>*Question?*</u>

6: Time how valuable is it to you? Think about that, we will get back to this. I Left Some room for you to write your answer.

Moral Of the Story!

7: There's no more right Than Good Moral! So, ask yourself...Does it feel right to you? Would you allow that into your life accept that in your peace? will it give you peace? All very serious questions to disregard the thought is ignorant because truth is we always can tell what is morally correct and what is morally wrong. The choice is always free. but the knowing intuitively is alive and very vibrant. We call this a gut feeling. Sometimes it takes guts to trust your gut!

Take The Shot!

8: Be acceptant of Challenges! Not on being the challenger! Although it is ok to push for good even in others as some would say I see great potential so, I push you! Make sure that you yourself have overcome and risen to such challenges. Also, to accept a challenge in life not because you want to prove something to someone No! Accept the challenge because it is a way to enhance knowledge or growth in whatever area the subject. That is the difference between a purposeful challenge and wasted time. Do not defeat an entity, it is only a belief system. You are in no way weak or incapable of anything!

Let's Give Thanks!

9: Say Thank You! For Everything! When we awaken in the morning throughout the day and before we shut our eyes! To be thankful even when things are less favorable shows strength and optimism. It lets the universe know that you understand its laws and systems, it allows for an invisible mercy and for it to shift to allow better days! or opposite remove patterns that are not benefiting you in its time of flow. Do not let the idea of sunny days take away the respect for the rainy days which is so necessary for growth! it is a wash and rinse cycle in which is very important to clear out and allow those sunny days to shine bright and finish the polish after the wash! In other words, you need the bad days to teach! and the good days to understand and reflect. Besides, what's a great story if there is no villain? Even in fairy tales we sympathize with such things because we learn to understand why they act as so and what purpose they serve in the plot they are in fact The lesson! Most lessons are free but if we ignore them well, we will find that later on it will cost more to learn it!

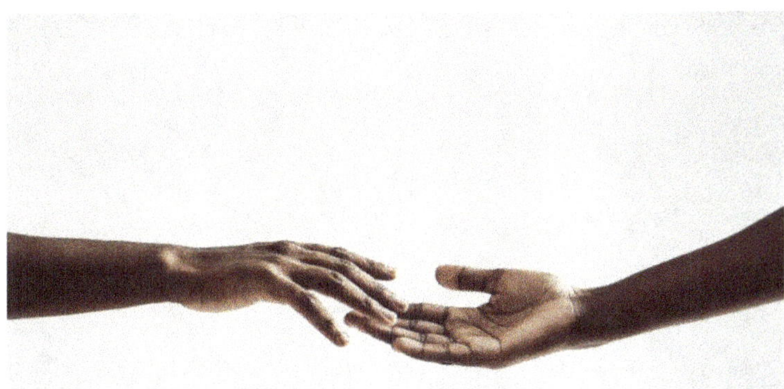

10: Be YOU! You play such an important part in the circle of life! We need you! your unique make and model! You were designed for purpose your words your charisma your point of views and you have been employed by the universe to perform such duties with love and light. It keeps the world circling at a pace that allows for an ebon flow. Think about it! If no 2 individuals are alike, then that makes you 1 of 1! We can't get that back in someone else or from someone else! It is important that you understand you have a very important role! We often see people become carbon copies of what they feel is a better mask than their authentic default. That's a shame it serves no good! It is ok to be inspired by others, that's the point! but we should never try and become the other! We simply learn the things we need and adapt and apply them as necessary throughout life. Remember we are evolving every day we must learn everyday there is no right way except good morals! So, no one individual is above another, it's a system of knowledge exchange! The challenge is will you water for growth or rob the garden? so are you helping or picking every pretty flower that blooms? If you like the flower keep watering and let the sunshine and give strength show others the flower and how your unique gifts have contributed to its growth and then allow their inspiration to give to it as well. Now we have multiple flowers just off one seed! See how that worked.

<u>Life is Just an Incredible Gift!</u>

The Breakdown of #6

11: So back to time, how do you define it? What is it worth? Beauty or destruction? Wasteful or cherished, appreciated or owed? See we are only never granted the time. It is borrowed a loan in which we have the freedom to do wonderful, extraordinary life altering things! Most of us, even you! waste a lot of time as if we will ever get that back! In fact, it's sad to not fill that up with ideas and memories of positive encounters with different people and situations. Instead, we allow time to sit like empty cups allowing for most of them to be filled with rain which leaves no room for anything to transpire out them. To use time to its best purpose is to push through with good intent, allow for others to fill add to your time with positive things. wasted time is allowing negative things to consume that! You never get that time back so the chances of correcting that can always be done but never and I do mean Never do you get that same time back! So, take time seriously! Devaluing time is disrespectful and quite selfish!

The Main Ingredient

12: Love! You should try and do all things with Love as the main driver! After all it was with great love in which you were created! Even if in life you were not shown this in your earliest of years you should and must understand you would not be here if love was not the influence on your being! remember You are an employee for the ebon flow of life! You have great importance, and your role should be respected not just by others but by you first! It is only through the notion of love that we see and give the most positive change! It is literally the antidote for forward movement! and endless possibilities. in adversity and indifference, we must always lead with Love! and to start we must in fact Love thy self! Only then do we become immune to resistance to it. and almost a superhero to those who oppose it.

<u>*Say Cheese!!!*</u>

13: Smile! It's the only infection we want to catch! and you should want to give! A smile makes you approachable! It lets people know you are a safe person! and to attract healthy harmonious relationships if we start with a genuine smile, we learn to tell the difference between a real smile and a false smile. false smiles come with sneaky and negative intentions. learn the difference by practicing genuine smiles. Every day you should wake up and smile! Try it I bet your laugh a little to yourself that's ok that's your reflection acknowledging its safe and happy! You are safe and happy. that bubble throughout the day isn't an all access but will allow those dressed for the party free entry!

<u>*Let's Be Real!*</u>

14: Be Honest! Start with yourself except the things you are already blessed with! Not with the disappointment of what you do not have! Happiness is having what you have, not what you want! Don't play the dealer in your life! Let things come and go as the universe sees fit! It's easier that way! less stressful the more options one sees the harder the choice! don't over burden your mind with wants to make the terms simple buy placing what you need into the air rather than the desires of what you see everyone else having! Remember you are 1 of 1! does not matter the brand of shoe but how one wears it! take this method and apply it to everyday living and watch the weight of criticism and the measures to fit in drop immensely. Because what did we say earlier those who mind don't matter and those that matter doesn't mind! Go on, try it!

<u>*No One Knows It All!*</u>

15: Arrogance is Jealously! I'm sorry but it is! See Arrogance is the notion that only you reign superior in thinking! Wrong! it proves your jealous because you can only limit your mind to that unlike other people who are open an accept the notion that people have their own minds and are gifted the same will to think freely and formulate their own difference of opinions and thoughts about things in the matters of everyday life! How foolish do you look projecting the fact that you don't understand that! and why not wonder why that is? Being arrogant draws people away. It's ok, we all we understand you could be right but have you no room for other explanations and breakdowns of why they think they could be right and find common ground! all fine but not a good recipe for respect and friendships! Don't be sloppy, it looks meek and unrefined. No one likes a know it all, it's like a pimple with no head, just big red and ugly also painful and very unwanted.

<u>*You Have a Friend in You!*</u>

16: Be your own friend first! don't chase don't Begg! For only in the company of yourself do you learn the proper etiquette for formulating friendships and healthy connections, you learn more about yourself by spending the time to get to know what yourself really is about. If you don't learn that first, you risk the chance of being oversaturated by the identities of those around you. This can cause great confusion over time, the term lost myself has been applied by some people who have in fact no knowledge of who they are based on the overindulgence of people pleasing and the need to fit in by wearing the false mask other than the default they were designed with! If one can find joy in sitting alone at a park full of people reading or just sitting enhancing the mind smiling because well, we are happy the universe gets a signal it begins to illuminate you sending a signal to those who have progressed in that chapter of self-awareness! thus sending the right people at the right time in an equal ebon flow of life! You are never alone, that's just an idea to scare your thoughts from evolving and a slow dancing partner with Negativity!

<u>No Deadlines</u>

17: Make sense of what you can remember there is no deadline! But do be mindful of your time! Fill it with grander thoughts apply happy vibrations self-awareness and self-love! Don't put too much on your plate, that's gluttony and you'll end up with a stomachache! so pace yourself a little today save some for tomorrow remember time is borrowed! Lead with Love be thankful for you! This is what your reflection is really saying to YOU!

Healthy Living Starts Now!

 Wow you're doing a great job! You're almost unrecognizable!

Removing all those toxic negative thought patterns has sure lightened the pressures of everyday life. Now there's more room to learn, grow and expand this new knowledge. Healthy living is just one of our superpowers, let's keep going, there's so much more!

Thank you so much for your help! Now pass what you learned, how you have grown and show them the way! There's no Greater Gift than being able to help others and no greater power than be able to recognize just how important and needed we are! May you always be lifted forever gifted and remember to leave the light on for those in the dark!